7 YEARS OF
DANCING WITH
Lust

Deandra Evans

ISBN 978-1-63961-244-4 (paperback)
ISBN 978-1-63961-245-1 (digital)

Christian Faith Publishing, Inc.
832 Park Avenue
Meadville, PA 16335
www.christianfaithpublishing.com

Printed in the United States of America

CHAPTER 1

Meeting Lust

I read somewhere that love is a deep feeling of affection that you have for another person. It's a lasting attraction that goes beyond the surface and turns into emotional attachment. *Lust*, on the other hand, is basically a physical attraction that leads to an overwhelming feeling of sexual desires, thanks to a rush of hormones. Well, isn't that something! You see, lust can be many things to many people, but for me, it was so much more. For me, it came in one form. *Lust* was a *beautiful, tall, golden-brown, toned brother with tattoos*. He had a smile that was out of this world, and not to mention, he had a vibe that I liked. He was also charming and charismatic, always knowing just what to say and just what to do.

It all began on a sunny day in October—our ninth grade year. I was playing ball like I usually did back then. After playing around, I decided to sit down on my porch and just chill. That's when I looked up, and there he was, strolling my way with my classmate, Mike. He was the most handsome thing I had ever seen. If I were a cartoon, my eyes would have jumped out of my head and ran straight to him. I was instantly mesmerized from our instant attraction to each other. I could tell that even my sister was a fan of this union between us. He looked me over with his beautiful golden-brown eyes, and I knew I had him hooked. If truth be told, I was seriously serving a vibe. I wore basketball shorts and a fitted, canary-yellow V-neck that made my mahogany-chocolate skin pop. My hair was cut into a beautiful bob, and it went perfectly with my tomboy yet girlish attitude—a look that showed I'm cute and fun, not doing too much for attention. It worked! I just knew I had him and he had me also.

At that time, we seemed inseparable. Sadly though, our union was cut short due to me moving away, and at that time, that was the hardest goodbye. During ninth grade summer, going into tenth grade, we reconnected. I went back to my hometown to visit family and spend time with my godmother. Lust would soon find me via Myspace. I now know that Lust was drawn to me like a moth to a flame. Honestly, I was drawn to Lust and what I thought he was. I came to learn that Lust would break up and leave me for many reasons unknown to me. It was like a game of cat and mouse, and I wanted to catch him.

Finally, the roller-coaster rides in our relationship got extremely old, and I just decided to get off. We would break up for nothing and be back together months later. I was over it. The back-and-forth thing was too much for my young nerves at that time. So during my last year of high school, we decided to be friends. Besides that, I was really focused on graduating early. In order to do that, I had to combine my eleventh grade and twelfth grade years. So I really needed to focus on graduating alone—no distractions. We actually grew to be good friends—so I thought. It seemed like everything worked better that way. I told Lust my deepest secrets and things that I did, and he did the same with me. We shared all of our ups and downs in our personal relationships, but outside of that, we grew closer.

Coming into my beauty college year, I decided to give love a try elsewhere. Well, needless to say, Lust wasn't having it. I got engaged to Mr. Right now, and Lust issued me a fake congratulations. I could literally feel the sarcasm in his text. "Congrats."

As I waited at the crowded Florida airport, reading the text, all I could really focus on was Lust being upset with me for moving on. Here I was, waiting to see my Mr. Right now with Lust on my brain. I tried my best to focus on my current relationship because well, he wanted me and I thought I wanted him. I mean, who wouldn't want a muscular Mexican half-Italian marine. He was medium height and had the cutest baby face you've ever seen. Little did I know I was using him to rid myself of Lust once and for all.

Lust had many failed attempts trying to get me back. Finally, I was caught right back in the ever-so-sticky spider web. Mr. Right now and I's relationship was on the rocks. He was extremely unsupportive of anything concerning me. There would be times when I needed to confide in him and he'd basically say that he didn't want to hear it. By this, I was extremely upset and was sitting in a steamy bath, trying to soak my issues away, when—I received a call from Lust.

Feeling like I just needed a night out, I obliged Lust and agreed to hang out with him. I was literally so excited that I hurried out of the bathtub and put on my tightest skinny jeans, with a cute blouse that revealed my tattoos. I even threw on some sandals to show off my freshly painted toes. I anxiously stepped outside the front door and walked nervously down the apartment stairs to his white car. When I opened the car door, there he was—just as handsome as I remembered. He immediately looked up at me, flashing that big, million-dollar smile in my direction. Man, he sure was looking good, and I knew Lust could give me a good time—and he did.

CHAPTER 2

Conceiving with Lust

Officially, Lust and I decided to be together, and now we could. Nothing and no one could break us up. During that time, he lived in Fort Worth, but that never stopped him from visiting me. Whenever Lust wanted to make my eyes roll back in my head or my toes curl, he knew just how to find me. On many occasions, I'd follow him out of town. Lust knew I had a need, and it wanted to meet that need.

Soon, the traveling and distance became too much for Lust and I to handle. He moved back home where I was just so that he could be closer to me. I felt like it was just for me, but honestly, Lust wanted something from me as well. No one tells you that *lust* will suck the life right out of you and leave you feeling used up. They surely don't tell you it's a temporary scratch for that temporary itch. Lust was willing to do whatever it took to see me. He'd walk in the rain, sleet, and etc. just to be with me. I felt like he really loved me—yeah, don't confuse love with a good time.

Six months into the relationship, as we grew closer, we discovered we were expecting a baby. I was scared and excited, which made me welcome the challenge of becoming a new mother. He, on the other hand, seemed like he was excited but, in time, would show he wasn't ready at all. As the months went by and my belly grew bigger, Lust became scarce. He seemed to spend less and less time with me, unless it was to fulfill his wants and needs. In those months, I started to feel alone. Lust no longer had a need for me, and I knew it was because I was pregnant.

The connection between Lust and I was fading drastically. So much so that I decided to break up with him. Things between us just wasn't clicking anymore. He wouldn't really ever ask about the baby—he'd only be concerned about me. My mind had already changed to the *us* setting, but he was stuck solely on *he* and *I*.

So the day came when I mustered up some courage to tell a lie saying, "I lost the baby. You're off the hook." But then again, I was like, *I can't speak that on my child's life*. So I thought of the multitude of things to say so that we'd be done with each other. I was sitting on a gray suede couch, trying to end my relationship with the father of my child. Just then, Mr. Persuader called me. Mr. Persuader is related to Lust, so I should have figured that he'd advocate for me to stay with Lust. So foolishly, I began to pour out my heart to Mr. Persuader about leaving Lust once and for all. Mr. Persuader—being the crafty, little persuader that he is—convinced me to stay. He began to tell me all these great plans of Lust wanting to marry me. My ears started ringing—by this time, all I could think about was marrying Lust. How stupid!

One day, Lust called me and said our family should meet to see if they will like each other. Like an idiot, I eagerly agreed because I thought, *This is all for the baby*. I mean, we were going to be connected by this child, so it's only right that we meet. We decided to meet at Chili's because Lust had a thing for that "two for twenty bucks." Around the table sat his mother, her girlfriend, my mom, my dad, and my sister—we couldn't have been happier.

After a successful dinner, Lust and I decided to have some alone time, and for those of you who are not sure—yes, I do mean sex. As we were in the middle of this alone time, Lust got the nerve to ask me to marry him. I immediately declined his offer, leaving him somewhat upset. I explained to him that I didn't want to be married to him because we were having a baby. I really wanted real love. He proclaimed that he'd show me that he was serious about it. Honestly, I felt like I justified my no. I mean, the entire nerve of him to ask for my hand without so much as a ring. Who was he kidding, right?

CHAPTER 3

Committing to Lust

There would be two more times that I turned down a marriage proposal from Lust. By the final time, I started to believe he really wanted to marry me. I was living in Temple, and Lust was living with some family in Waco area.

It was July 4, and my mom and I decided to drive down to Waco for the holiday. I didn't know if it was just because I was expecting, but I could smell barbecue everywhere. Honestly, I had the nose of a greyhound while I was pregnant. I alerted Lust that I'd be in town and asked my mom to pick him up. When we arrived in town, I was extremely eager to see him. My mom picked him up, and we all went over to my grandma's house to celebrate the festivities.

Lust and I were sitting on the couch when he asked me to join him outside at my grandma's house. He stood up and grabbed my hand, leading me right out the front door. We made our way to the backyard, and he began to initiate some alone time. Here we were—dumb as ever getting well-deserved mosquito bites all over our behinds, legs, and etc. I mean, what did we expect having a quickie outside? I won't lie—I really did do some stupid things for and with Lust.

After that, we went for a walk, and Lust began to mention marriage again. The funny thing about Lust was that he always knew what buttons to push to sway me into doing what he wanted. Also, Lust knew my desires for my family to be whole. So he began telling me that he wanted me and our child to carry his name. He also told

8

me that he loved me more than anything in the whole world. And so, I finally agreed to become Mrs. Lust.

We decided that we were going to get married on July 21. He chose the date because he said he wanted us to do it the Sunday after we were going to find out our baby's gender. So we began calling and telling our families the good news. We had plenty of naysayers and people who thought we shouldn't even be thinking about marriage. Maybe we should have listened to those naysayers. I don't know, but that didn't stop us.

So finally, the day approached, and it was time for us to find out the gender of our baby. I was also excited because we were getting married in a few days. At least that was what I thought!

On my way to my doctor's appointment, I received a phone call from him stating, "We should change the wedding date. My mom is going gambling this weekend and wanted to know if we could pick another date."

Well, needless to say, I became upset because here I was feeling like our wedding was not more important than her gambling. To me, it was a big red flag that he'd never put me first. I expected Lust to forsake all others and make me priority. I considered calling the whole thing off, so I talked it over with my mom. She told me it won't hurt to wait another week because he really wanted his mother there. So I ignored my giant red flag and called it a compromise. I mean, that's what you do when you love someone, right? After talking about it on several occasions, I still agreed to marry Lust.

The night before the wedding, he spent the night with me at my parents' house. On July 28, 2013, I woke up nervous and excited because I knew today was the big day. I was not sure if it's the butterflies or the baby kicking like crazy—all I knew was I was nervous. Finally, after an awesome Sunday service, it was time for the ceremony or lack thereof. My mom and sister walked me down the aisle. As they were walking me down, it seemed like I was getting superhot, like I was heading into a sauna. I looked up and focused on Lust. He was sweating like a sinner in church.

As we began to exchange our vows, Lust began to cry very hard. It was like he couldn't utter the words "till death do us part." Each word he attempted to utter, he choked on. Little did I know each bullet that fell from his brown eyes were tears of sorrow. Those tears were for everything he knew he couldn't give up. Lust was trapped and didn't want to be. Me staring at my significant other with natural eyes felt like it was beautiful to see him cry on our special day. Boy was I in for years' worth of truth behind those tears.

After we said "I do," we were unaware of the seven-year dance that awaited us. Here I was thinking blind that I will live happily ever after with my dream guy. Life with Lust was about to get seriously real. It would soon prove to be the biggest eye-opening experience I've ever had.

After the wedding, I experienced a little family drama. His grandma decided to hit me on the back of my head while I was eating. I mean, who does this type of stuff? So my mom, being the wonderful parent that she is, hit that old lady right on the back of her head. She then assured her that it would be in her best interest not to ever touch me like that again.

Months later, we were living in our own home when Lust received a visit from old flames. She came by my house with her beautiful green eyes and the golden curls. The entire nerve of this heifer to only be wearing a one-half blouse in mini shorts. She was showing off her high yellow skin tone. I just knew she had to have lost her mind coming over to my house like that. The funny thing was when I mentioned her visit to Lust, the idiot told me that I should have awaken him so he could say hi. I honestly could have slapped fire from his face. Lust was so disrespectful sometimes. Surely, he didn't think that old flames coming by our home to see him was okay. Arrogance and rudeness were something he wore well often.

Once he woke up, I confronted him about the situation, and he flipped it on me. He made it seem like I was making a big deal out of nothing. If truth be told, I wasn't reacting enough in moments like that. I was the one letting him treat me the way he was, and he was only doing what I allowed. What I mean by that ladies is that we set the standard of how a man should treat us. Just be careful of how you let a man treat you. He remained the disrespectful Lust who I chose to still love or, should I say, lust for.

CHAPTER 4

Born to Lust

After nine hours of labor—sweating, crying, and throwing up—we welcomed our first son, Bubs. I had a room full of supporters and one unwanted guest. The reason she came was only to insult me and inform me that I looked unattractive during labor. How ironic is it that you're supposed to be supportive but you're the opposite? Truth be told, Bubs probably didn't want to come out so he wouldn't have to see her face. I was literally in labor for the first time in my life, and this crazy chick expected me to look like a movie star. At least I had a reason for looking crazy—what was her excuse? The crazy thing was I did not invite her to be there and it was not even remotely pleasant having her there.

I later determined that she was a spectator. You know—to make sure the baby was really his and then she'd leave and report back to his family. A day later, it was time to go home with the baby. At the hospital, Lust stared at our baby with love in his eyes. So naturally, I thought our little family was going to be great. I could see all the great things Lust and Bubs would do together. I had so much faith in Lust. Thinking about it now, that was truly a laugh. Let me be clear, lust is something attached to the person—not the actual person. You see, I had faith in the person's ability to be great, but I was dealing with lust who was attached to him.

Lust would be gone all day, helping his sister with her kids, and would come back sleepy and unhelpful to me. He'd go back to work and come back doing the same thing all over again. On some days, he'd get off work and go straight to his sister's house and I wouldn't see him until it was time for him to go to work—so, little to no time together at all most days.

Income tax season came around, and I decided that since I never asked for anything, I would ask for something that I really wanted us to have. I wanted us to have our wedding rings—considering we didn't have any and were married. Lust, being who he was, stated that if I allowed him to get his $700 PlayStation then he'd get our rings, which by the way cost $100 altogether. Now I was not realizing the selfishness of Lust, and maybe, I was being naïve about it. I felt like I was being appreciative that we were getting rings because it was clear he didn't want rings. You see, I chose to see what I wanted to see even though Lust presented who he was. So I took owner-ship of what transpired because I kept allowing it. Mya Angelou said this. "When they show you who they are, believe them." Someone should've added, "Believe them the first time." Well, here I was—young, foolish, and in lust with Lust.

When Bubs turned four months old, we decided to move to Fort Worth, Texas. First, we lived with his family, and after a short while, we had a pad of our own. Life seemed to be taking off for Lust and me. Never did I know this move would cause my spirit to suffer greatly. Me seeing with my physical eyes saw it as a great, fresh start. How naïve of me to think this was something good. Lust's original plan was to move by himself and then he'd send for Bubs and me. That made me feel like a burden, but I said, "Maybe I'm overreact-ing." I always checked my feelings on things even if I felt it strongly in my gut. Sometimes, we want what we want without weighing the pros and cons. We never think of seeking God about it, then we wonder why we're so miserable. The move to Fort Worth unleashed many dark things.

CHAPTER 5

Unsuccessful Split from Lust

Things went to a whole new form of ugly between Lust and me. No one told me that it had other attachments like addiction and infidelity. Yes! The spirits traveled in packs. Maybe I always knew that he did those things—I just refused to acknowledge the other attachments. You know, there really is such a thing as being blind to what's going on around you. So I was really choosing to live in oblivion—only focusing on the potential of the person. You can't push someone to greatness if they don't have the desire to be there.

One day, Lust came home at seven in the morning, smelling like weed. His eyes were so low that he looked like he was sleeping while standing. He got off work the evening before but didn't come home until the next day. Here I was trying to be a good wife, and my supposed spouse didn't even respect me enough to come home—and at a decent time at that. How disrespectful can you possibly get? That angered me so much that I could feel heat and steam coming out of my ears. Every time I closed my eyes, I saw pure red. Now I decided to muster up the courage to ask him, "Do you even still want to be married to me?"

Lust looked at me dead in my eyes and said, "No, not really," and walked off.

His eyes glazed unkindly, matching his words. Hearing those words put me in an immediate three-day hell. I cried those three days, and I went to stay at a friend's house with our son trying to cope. Lust carried on like nothing happened. I couldn't eat or sleep from feeling so lost inside. On the third day, I called the only people I knew I could count on. They prayed for me and assured me they'd be there for me. My mom and dad are two God-fearing people that I knew could get a prayer through. They agreed to come get me and take me home with them to Temple, Texas. My cousin's wedding was that weekend, so they agreed to pick me up—I'd just have to wait until then. So I tried my best to snap out of it because I knew with some spiritual guidance, I will get through this. Boldly I told Lust that I was leaving and he'll never have to worry about me again.

Lust, being a crafty manipulator that he was, said, "I've decided not to divorce you. I don't want anyone doing to you and for you what I can do. Go spend the week with your parents and come back when you've calmed down."

Right then, I should've slapped Lust into a new planet, but I didn't because I was focused on going home. The funny thing about Lust is that once you try to get away, it will use every trick possible to keep you. Lust said it clearly as the day—he did not want me with anyone else nor did he want someone else doing what he could with me. It was selfish, and I know that now.

For a whole month, I was living in Temple—away from him—and I've decided I didn't want to go back. I even went as far as to admit to Lust that I didn't trust him to care for me. The fun fact is—Lust doesn't care for anyone except the need.

One night, I went to church, and my pastor at that time assured me that I should go back home. No offense to people in ministry leadership but stop telling people things out of flesh. If God didn't tell you to say it, then you shouldn't say it. Anyway, days after, Lust called me with a sob story of how he misses me. He promises that he'll do right by me this time. Lust went so far as to try to convince my parents that he wanted me home. Then two nights before it was time for them to bring me, I got an urge to check Lust's activities—it was another big red flag not to go back, but I wanted to be in my own space. So here I was preparing to come home, and Lust was cyber cheating. So I bluffed and said I was going to divorce Lust because he obviously didn't want me back. Stupidly though, I went back way too early to him anyway and grew to hate him. It became unbearable. I no longer loved him. I only cared about what he could do for me. If truth be told, I wanted to be in my own home so bad that I ignored my signs to divorce him.

CHAPTER 6

Second Born and Turning Point

Lust and I seemed to be doing better in our relationship. I began a new job, and so did he. We moved into our own place, and all was great. A little before my birthday, I was pregnant with our second child after having a miscarriage. The crazy thing is the miscarriage was supposed to end in a D&C, but I didn't do it. Lust and I seemed to be tighter than ever clicking like old times. I had some red flags then, but I chose to overlook them. Lust often proved to be very neglectful of me and our baby. Like this one day when I was at work and it was time for me to go home. He knew my schedule was 8:00 a.m. to 4:00 p.m., and he forgot to pick me up. Here I was expecting him to be there and ended up waiting over an hour to leave from work. I ended up calling my aunt after many failed attempts trying to reach him. When my aunt came to get me, she was angry and fussing about Lust neglecting me and our son. She explained that he was still sleeping on the couch and had never changed our son's Pampers and he now had a diaper rash. He just sat in a poopy Pampers while his dad slept the day away. Lust really got on my last nerve sometimes, and my family felt the same way.

Lust got off from working a double shift one morning, and I could tell he was tired. He decided to drive me to work with our son in the car. I told him I loved him and asked him to promise to go straight back to our home and just go to bed. Lust had this thing about having other people watch our son, so he didn't have to. So like normal, instead of going home, he drove to his grandma's house, which is farther away. Randomly, I got a call from Lust, and I missed it. I felt this urge to call him back, and when I did, all I heard was sirens in the background and my baby crying. By this time, I was in full panic mode. He began to tell me that he did not go home like I asked him to. He explained to me that he drove to his grandma's house so his aunt could watch our son while he slept. Typical! When he made it to her street, he fell asleep at the wheel and hit a telephone pole. The car was completely totaled. Don't get me wrong—I know it wasn't intentional. I know life happens, but I really wished he would've listened to me that day. His sister picked me up from work and rushed me to the hospital to meet them. We walked in and found Lust sitting on the hospital bed, looking like a wounded animal. All thanks to God—when I searched the room, my son was up and running around like nothing happened. All he had was a cut on his chin. Lust's only concern was that I might be mad at him for endangering our son. I won't lie—I thanked God that Sunday for keeping my family from the grave.

Getting to work became hard without a car, and due to the accident, Lust lost his job. I was already on the verge of losing my job due to me dealing with morning sickness. Lust grew tired of not making more money and decided to start driving trucks for a living. Like a good, little wife, I supported him and helped find a company to go to.

I told him, "It'll be hard being apart, but we'll get through this."

Finally, he landed a gig in Fort Worth area, so we moved with his family. At this time, I was unable to see the pattern Lust and I were creating. Instability became our entire foundation. Well, needless to say, we ended up moving back to Waco with a family friend after hopping from two other homes. So here I was going here, there, and everywhere with our family.

The time was drawing near, and it was almost time for me to have our second child, Blithe. Lust, at this time, had been on the road for months now, and we'd only see him on weekends. I had my last doctor's appointment on a Thursday morning. I called him to let him know that the doctor said the baby would be here by the weekend. He ended up coming home that Friday evening, and my labor kicked off the next morning. As I was in early labor, Lust slept soundly. Now that I think about it, he was always not helpful when I'm in early labor. Honestly, I couldn't see past my own pain. Lord knows those contractions sucked. After two hours of labor, Blithe was born. I was excited because it definitely seemed like everything was turning out great. I just knew that we were happy again.

During our six-week recovery time, I discovered that Lust was cyber cheating again. It always seemed to hurt worse because I thought things were good between us. Lust was entertaining three different ladies and felt like it was okay. He'd say it was only for conversations.

"I'm your wife, and you should be talking to me or Jesus."

At this point, it seemed like Lust got a kick out of hurting me emotionally. I began to believe that, maybe, I was not enough. Lust promised he'll change again, and we moved forward blind. Honestly, we were not moving forward blind. Actually, we were running repeatedly into the relational wall that we never seemed to get past—cheating! One epic relational stumbling block.

One day, we went to visit Mr. Persuader, and it was a lot of drama over his mom's house. Lust's mother was there, and she was tripping. I felt like Lust's mother was dogging him, but I wasn't sure why. She seemed to be really extra all because his ex-girlfriend was sitting in the living room with me. We were at his aunt's house, and his ex-girlfriend—old flame—was going to do her hair. I wasn't bothered at all. Years later, I would learn that Lust had a physical affair with another woman from out of the state and his mom thought it was his ex. Truly, I felt like his mom should have told me right then and there. I guess some people aren't big on morals.

After a year of trying to get a place of our own, we finally found one in Bellmead. By now, we have a three-year-old and a one-year-old. Life was truly going smoothly. We were enjoying having our own home, and everything seemed perfect.

It's like we would experience the highest highs and then, out of nowhere, the lowest of lows.

CHAPTER 7

The Downward Spiral

A month or two after moving into our new home, we discovered we were expecting baby number three. I was working for the marketplace, and he was a bay driver for a great company. Everything was running smoothly until Lust lost his job. When that happened, I had to step up. You see, I wanted to turn this negative into a positive situation. I assured him everything would be okay. I assured him it'll work out for us—kind of. With him being home now, we wouldn't have to pay for a babysitter anymore. Here I was trying to comfort Lust's ego and his pride. Also, I was trying to be a supportive wife to my supposed husband. So as my belly got bigger and my hormones changed, I remained as rational as possible. I mean, someone had to stay positive or we'd all fall apart.

After a few weeks, Lust got a little night job. He would make me wake him up at midnight to take him to work. We lived on the second floor, so that meant we were going downstairs to the car with two sleeping kids. Then after I'd drop him off, I'd come back and have to carry those same two sleeping kids up the stairs to our apartment with my big belly. He didn't care that my sleep was interrupted. Then by 6:00 a.m., I had to be up again, carry our sons downstairs to the car, and pick him up. Oh yeah, and I had to make it to my job by 7:00 a.m. I stayed, making sacrifices for Lust, but I would get put on the back burner often. Eventually, he stopped working at the night job because he overslept a lot. (Sidebar: I was his alarm clock and would always have to wake him up for work.) I took on extra hours at my job and did so while suffering horrible morning sickness. There would even be times where Lust wouldn't even bring me a lunch to work.

I remember one day—I was about a little over four months along, and I asked him to bring me some food. He'd spend all day on his PS4 and wouldn't really be watching the kids or paying attention to anything. He said he would, but then he'd forgot, and I wouldn't know it, so I would be at work waiting. My lunch was an hour long, and by this time, we lived only five minutes away, so I wasn't sure why he hadn't come. I began to get so upset that I started to cry. I had to walk to the Burger King with only four bucks to my name. All I was able to get was a little chicken sandwich or I think it was called little chicky. I was truly upset for the remainder of the day. I blamed it on my hormones, but it was truly much more. There will be times where Lust would forget me at work. He'd say he thought I told him a random later time and that was why he was late.

Lust had his own particular lusts. He had a lust for weed, more money, and entertainment from other women. Lust was never satisfied. One day, we got into a heated argument about him entertaining someone late at night. You see, Lust went out every weekend with friends or family. Clubs, pool halls, or smoke sessions—you name it. That's where he had to be. He made it a priority, and we argued about it all the time. That's when it happened—he grabbed my arm. Due to my past, I really hated that type of aggressive behavior. So big belly and all, I snatched away from him and started to walk off. Lust felt like that was disrespectful and decided to push me. Well, luckily, I was by the kitchen wall, so I couldn't fall. We then had a screaming match, and I told him to leave—more like I yelled, "Get your stupid self out of my house!"

To me, he was stupid for that and could've hurt me or our unborn daughter. Lust was becoming more and more okay with disrespecting me. He no longer seemed to care that he was crossing the line.

Sometime in May, my job shut down and Lust had a great job with excellent pay. So things were seeming to be turning around.

Go to these amazing UPS and then hit these horrible lows. It was a never-ending dance of back-and-forth. Even in those good times, I lacked love and quality time that I desired from Lust. If it wasn't for my two sons, I would have been lonelier than I already was.

At the end of my pregnancy, Lust was taking weeks off from work, which I thought was for me. I mean, that was what he told me, but his game got more attention than I did. I got his attention when he wanted some alone time. So while he was home, we decided to go for a swim after he smoked. We got the boys ready and drove to the apartment pool. The day was superhot. It was almost like the sun warmed the pool for us. It was a nice, clear, blue water and so very relaxing too. I got in and played with our boys while their dad was having swim races with Mr. Undercover Creeper. I call him that because he secretly held feelings for me that I could not return. I began water aerobics and that was when my contractions started.

Finally, when things really kicked off, we went inside the house for a shower and decided we wanted ice cream. All the while, I was having contractions. We went to Walmart and up and down our apartment stairs. The contractions got close like eight minutes apart, and right now, I was sitting up on a big, red birthing ball. I was bouncing up and down, rocking back and forth, and making circles while sitting on this big, red ball, trying to ease my pain. Instead of helping me, Lust got on his PlayStation and put on his headphones.

He told me, "Just let me know when you're ready to go to the hospital."

Just the type of helpfulness you need when you're in labor! My contractions intensified, so I began to say, "Let's leave now."

We dropped the boys off, and I made sure to hug and kiss them, assuring them I was okay as I was in pain. We got to the park and started to walk the baby down a little more before leaving for the hospital. After three hours of excruciating pain, feeling like my insides were about to rip, at nine thirty-two at night, she came. We were surrounded by friends and family, and it should have been the best moment ever.

After my family left, that's when things went downhill. The medicine wore off, and I was informed by the nurses that I could not eat because the kitchen was closed. So I asked Lust to bring me some food. He left and didn't come back until four something the next morning and didn't have any food for me. He said he went home to smoke and got money from his grandma to go to McDonald's to get himself two chicken sandwiches.

The nerve of this fool to say, "I forgot to get you something. I ate one on the way here before getting pulled over for speeding and left the other in the car. You can have the one in the car if you want."

If it wasn't for the fact that I had just given birth and I was just not a ghetto person, I could have knocked him out. You would have thought that was clear enough for me to know that he didn't care enough about me. Well, it wasn't clear. I believe that marriages have ups and downs—times wouldn't be always perfect. I respected my vows to "death do us part," so I stayed. Little did I realize I was about to endure so much more.

When we were released to go home, everything was back to the same way it was. I had to adjust to life with a new baby and an almost four-year-old and a one-year-old. Life carried on normal for Lust. As a matter of fact, when we got home, the kids were hungry, so Lust had me make their food. Mind you, they were kids, so they ate messily. I was cleaning up instead of recovering from my newborn. He even left me with all three of the kids as I was crying because my body hurt. Lust decided he needed a smoke session with one of our neighbors. I was engorged, tired, and overwhelmed, dealing with a newborn and two toddlers. Lust hurried and got back on the road, leaving me to do it all. I'd sometimes have to take him to Hutchins for his job and then pick him back up on the weekends—all this while living in Waco and traveling with three kids constantly for him.

A month later from the day our daughter was born was our anniversary. I was super excited and wanted to do something special for him. I knew Lust wasn't doing anything for me because he was not romantic at all. I decided to buy some black-lace lingerie, just trying to feel sexy and be sexy for him. As I've said, I'm a mahogany-chocolate chick who, at this time, was very uncomfortable with my body. I mean, duh, I just had a baby a month ago. So I have a new mommy tummy, stretch mark, sand yet, I decided to try. I stepped out to show him what I have done as brave as I could be.

He took one look at me and said, "Black doesn't look good on black."

I walked back inside the bathroom and started to cry the hardest silent tears ever. I could not even believe the words he said to me. Who was this person that I married? Why would he say something like that to me? Then the jerk drove me back to the mall to get something else in a different color. He really didn't like what I picked. He purchased me a red-lace lingerie set, and he was so proud of himself. Somehow, I was still able to attempt to celebrate our anniversary. People say love is a powerful thing—well, so is lust.

A few days later, he left again, and I ended up getting really sick. I went to the hospital twice. The second time I was there, they told me I was going too fast and needed to slow down. I was physically exhausted, and my body started to reflect that. They wanted me to stay in the hospital, but as a mother of three, that was not realistic without help. They told me I was severely dehydrated and unable to breastfeed my newborn. I had a high-grade fever and the shakes. I could barely walk around because I was so weak from not being able to eat for the first week. I went home anyway but ended up at my aunt's house to recover. During that entire week, I suffered shakes, chills, high fevers, weight loss, lack of energy, and weakening muscles. I couldn't eat or drink. I told Lust about what was going on with me because he was on the road and didn't know. He began to tell me that's why he wanted to be home more—so he could help me. That second week, when I started to recover, he came home. I wasn't a hundred percent better. I walked like I just had a surgery. He arrived at my aunt's house extremely tired and had me, who was still in recovery, drive us all home. It was like he was purposely oblivious to what I needed. Where I was willing to sacrifice for him, Lust was willing to sacrifice me also. He was willing to use me to death, and I was oblivious to it.

Lust got the bright idea to quit his great-paying job and found something local. He said he was doing it to spend more time with us and to be closer. He has never spent time like that before. Here I was again thinking he'll finally improve. Lust got a chance at a local job in Dallas where we were trying to move, but he didn't get it. He quit his job before securing the possible one. As it turned out, he didn't get the new job because his habit showed up in a test. Then he got the bright idea to find another job in Dallas area. He told me he was going to leave me and the kids at the apartment we were getting evicted from. I took my children, and we went to stay with my parents, and he stayed with his stepmom. As I was living with my parents, he barely visited me and the kids. He rarely ever called because he said he was busy with whatever. He was always too busy to see us or talk to us.

To cut the long story short, we ended up living altogether with his stepmom. Everything seemed okay to the outside eye, but between me and Lust, there was a storm coming.

Lust had decided he wasn't sure if he wanted to be with me anymore. I knew something was wrong, but he'd never admit if there was someone else. His stepmom told me a few times that she could hear him screaming at me or talking crazy to me. It drove her nuts, and she let me know it every chance she got. She'd tell me several times that I should just leave because I didn't have to put up with that. It started to stress me out so badly that my hair was shedding. God knows I love my hair, so that was killing me. I had to get my hair cut off to make it healthy again. He asked me not to say anything to anyone when we're going through the possibility of a split. I was to act like nothing changed. Here he was stepping on what was left of my heart, and he expected me to just be okay with it. It was torture to me. I couldn't talk to my girls or my family about it. I had to carry on the façade that everything was all good. I managed to carry my broken pieces in silence. I started to fully become a shadow of who I was. I used to be full of life, and lately, it seemed like life was being sucked out of me.

Once he decided that he wanted to stay married to me, I just rolled with the flow. He wanted me to work and said he needed my help. The truth was, we were always without money, and it was because of his habit. Honestly, I wanted to work because I knew if I had money, we'd never be broke. The problem was, he would not watch the kids so I could contribute. In fact, I started working for Walmart for only two weeks when he made me quit. He claimed he couldn't handle our daughter because she was breastfed and struggling with going to formula. Honestly, he wouldn't watch her. He'd be on the PlayStation. It was like he was toying with my mind. He'd ask me to work, and I would, then he'd have me quit. At this point, I didn't know what he wanted from me.

CHAPTER 8

The Attempted Escape from Lust

I started going to church with my mom in DeSoto, trying to reconnect spiritually with God. I was so broken in many ways and was at my worst that I needed God. I was tired of pretending not to be broken and all the while falling apart. It happened that I wanted my children to finally see me whole. After some time, things started to turn around for me. Just when I was getting on the right track, my car stopped running properly. That didn't stop me though—it made it harder to get the church, but my mom was willing to help me get there, which meant she'd have to come from DeSoto to Arlington to get me, then back to DeSoto for us to go to church. I thank her so much for that.

Lust lost his job, leaving us unable to cover half of our expenses. His stepmom has had enough, and we ended up living with my parents again. Lust promised to stop smoking and planned to do better. He really did it—for a little while. By this time, I was growing extremely tired of his choices, taking things from our family. It was ruining us. So I needed him to get his act together. Lust ended up landing another great-paying job—thanks to my dad. My dad was always looking out for us on behalf of me. This job had him home only on Tuesday afternoon. As soon as it was Wednesday morning, he'd be gone again. When he actually got off on a Friday, maybe

Saturday, he'd make plans to go out with friends or play his game. Sometimes, he'd forget our date nights. He'd tell me I should have reminded him. People make time for the people and things they want to make time for. He was willing to spend time with everyone and everything except me and the kids. At least that was how it always felt.

Well, my parents started to notice, and it got old for them really quick. They eventually put him out of their house. He made it seem like they were picking on him, but the truth was, he was smoking again. He was disrespecting their home and neglecting me.

I got so fed up that I told Lust, "I've had it with you and this foolishness. I want a divorce."

CHAPTER 9

Trapped with Lust

Finally, I was free from Lust—so I thought. It became a spiritual thing because of how deep I was in. My soul was a temporary prisoner to Lust. I came to learn that we were indeed tied to each other. So when I began my process of moving on, it seemed to be working. Well, that was until I had the dream. You see, God gave me a gift, and he talked to me through my dreams.

In the dream, I was asleep when he walked in and leaned over the edge of the bed. He stared at me intently, looking just like the one I loved. Oh my gosh, here was Lust in its true form. Outside that dream, I was afraid, but inside, I was as oblivious as I seemed to be in reality.

So I started talking to him, asking, "Why are you just standing there?"

He began to smile this sinister smile up its face and said nothing. In the dream, my grandma was fussing at him, but it never broke its focus from me. I jumped out of my sleep, knowing the thing I saw was familiar but wasn't at the same time.

At that time, I didn't know who wore that evil grin. It would be two years later that I'd be able to put a name on what I saw. His name was Lust, and he wanted me to know who I was dealing with. He wanted me back to the point where he decided to appear to me. I was afraid that if I didn't go back, it would appear again, so I went back.

Few days later, Lust called and fear made me answer. I forgot that FEAR is *false* *e*vidence *a*ppearing *r*eal. So because it appeared real, I went back. Too many times, we're tricked back into the very thing God is pulling us from because of the false evidence appearing to be real. It's okay because even in my storm, God was in the midst.

So Lust proposed that we'd live together in his apartment like roommates—of course I had to except the fact that he openly smokes, drinks, and whatever else. The funny thing was, Lust had it to where it seemed like I was getting things my way, but the truth was, I was unknowingly still trapped.

CHAPTER 10

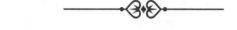

Stuck and Expecting

I'd do anything to make sure Lust's evil form didn't appear to me again. I agreed to move in with him to keep it from bothering me. Fun fact—whether I thought so or not, it was already bothering me. Somehow, we got back in the flow of how we used to be. We began to actually spend time together even though he still wanted me to divorce him. He wanted the benefits of having a wife without actually having one. Once again, I entered this crazy world of games and manipulations.

I began to get heavy into reading my Bible. I started reading so much that I had questions and long conversations about what I've read every day. Man, God is so awesome. I was amazed at all the things I was reading. There are stories of lust, war, love, betrayal, murder, etc. You name it, and it's probably in there. The story that stuck with me was the story of Delilah. If truth be told, we've all dealt with our own versions of Delilah in life.

I began to realize that the more I would read, the more God would talk and reveal things to me. He would show me more dreams or just talk to me clearly as the day.

After what we considered to be careful consideration, we decided to stay married. Shortly—and I do mean *shortly*—after, we discovered that we were expecting our last child. Lust showed his disappointment immediately by saying he needed to go smoke. I was crying because God knew I didn't want to be pregnant by him at all again. I continued to read my Bible and trusted God in this process because I knew he makes no mistakes.

During all of this, Lust quit his good-paying job. Now he was saying he wanted to be a stay-at-home dad. So I began working, and that didn't last very long because the car was acting up. Things were falling apart, but hey, we were together.

One day, I had this crazy dream that I was bleeding and about to lose my baby. I woke up scared, only to find out it wasn't just a dream—it was a warning. I was about to lose the baby for real. So I decided to go to the ER, and Lust told me to take our daughter with me. He stayed home with our two boys and his PlayStation. They explained to me that I was threatening to miscarry but it hasn't happened yet. I've had one before, so I didn't want to feel that pain again. So I went home worried that I was about to lose it for sure. They instructed me to come back on Sunday for more tests. I asked Lust to go with me to the hospital, and he said he will. When the day came, he informed me that he wasn't going with me. Then he told me to take our daughter with me and to just keep him posted. I wasn't surprised because he always did that to me. After a while of being there, Lust called me, saying he was hungry. No, of course he was not checking on me. I was so tired and hurting so bad that at this point, I checked out. Here I was worried about a baby that neither of us wanted. Maybe it's the mom in me, but I secretly loved the baby already. As a person who was married, I should've been overjoyed, but I wasn't. I was made to hate it. I mean, my marriage was barely hanging on—I didn't need another child. Honestly, I didn't hate that I was expecting. I hated who I was expecting with, and I knew what having another could mean for me—that I'd be doing all the work again.

When I got home, there was another woman sitting on my black couch with my supposed spouse. He left me lonely to entertain someone else. Fine, I get the message now!

You know, an apostle told me that he wasn't for me and that there was someone who would be. I was even showed a vivid dream of the faceless stranger. Yeah, well, I didn't believe I deserved better because I picked this person. Thank God my choice wasn't God's choice. He has someone better for me. It wouldn't be until March

2020 that I'd meet his choice for me. (So I thought.) Man, I sure did love who I thought was for me. That's for another story, but truly, God's choice will be the best choice.

As it turned out, I did lose the baby, and the doctors weren't sure if anything else needed to be done. Anyway, we ended up losing our apartment due to some serious hard times. We were going to move back to Waco and live with his family. So during this time of preparing for the move, God showed me dreams of my baby boy. He even let me hear myself say his name. God never stopped amazing me. He'd continue to talk to me while I was going through the chaos. I knew then we were expecting, and I was at peace this time.

We ended up living with Lust's family. The conditions weren't the best, but at least we had a place to lay our heads on. At the beginning of my pregnancy, things seemed to be going well. I was working and doing my part. Next thing I knew, morning sickness hit me hard. Eventually, Lust stopped smoking and got back on the road with my dad. Now I was seriously happy and thought I could see a change in my family. Things seemed to turn around for real this time.

An incident happened, and I knew things had only changed temporarily. Lust's male family member came into the room we were staying in. This man came in drunk and laid down right on me. Mind you, I was pregnant at this time and was lying on my back. So yeah, it wasn't easy to get up fast with the weight. By the way, he was lying sideways on me, so calm down. I guess when you think about it, he shouldn't have been on me anyway. Guess who got fussed at for this situation happening? Yeah, me! The door was closed, and I was lying down on my phone, minding my business. So I was like, *That's cool. I'll never tell you anything else concerning me. I'll take care of myself.*

Having my back was something he could never do—I should be used to that now. Wrong, some stupid part of me kept hoping he'd step up for me. Pregnancy with baby number four was really stressful. Nothing was going the way it should have. After the gender reveal for Zayv, things took a turn for the extreme worse—yes, again!

CHAPTER 11

Battle Against Lust

At the beginning of the 2019, we were just chilling at home when I asked about my water bottle. I asked him where he put it, and he claimed he didn't remember where he put it. Mind you, he was on the game, and he was distracted with his headphones on, talking to his buddies.

So then I said, "If you weren't going to do what I asked you to do, then why did you take it? You should've just let me do it myself."

I began to walk out the door when he grabbed my arm agressively. He stared at me with this angry look. Here was Lust presenting itself in the physical form now. I snatched away from him, and he got mad and pushed me into the dresser. I ended up hitting my shoulder. I got so angry I began to just fight back. In the room, there was this black couch, and as we were having this little battle, I remembered I was expecting—one of us had to stop or our baby (the one I was carrying) could get hurt. Clearly, he was not thinking at all because after that, he pinned me down on to the couch.

I yelled, "Get off me, stupid."

I mean, now I was really angry because I knew I was not safe and neither was our unborn child.

Once he finally stopped, he yelled at me, "Next time, don't talk to me like I'm a child."

I got even angrier and I was ready to leave. He went way too far this time. That was completely unnecessary to do all of that. The fact that he was willing to try to harm me in that moment became too much to handle. The rest of my pregnancy was so stressful.

Our oldest son ended up having a surgery. Lust did not show up. I took my big, pregnant self to surgery center with our son and stayed with him from start to finish. I got tired of being disappointed by his actions. It was one thing to leave me hanging but to leave our son hanging—I started to harden toward him. After two weeks of recovery, Bubs was doing great again.

During that time, I decided to sign the boys up for sports activities. Lust seemed to be a good soccer parent. Both of our boys played, but my youngest son, at that time, quit. Big and pregnant, I went to every game. I went to the doctor's office that morning before my oldest son's soccer tournament. The doctor told me I was dilated to three centimeter and he'd be coming really soon. So as I was at his game, I was having contractions—cheering through the pain. It was April 29, and it was late at night when my contractions finally kicked into early labor stage. His family house had stuff everywhere, so I couldn't get on the ground and use my birthing ball. We decided to go to my aunt's house and wait for my mom and sister to get there. Once they got into town and over to the house, my contractions became sporadic. Something seemed off, so we decided to go to the hospital to be sure. When we arrived, I felt this bolt of pain that took my breath away. From then on, my contractions intensified. Now I knew it was go time, but I needed to see if we were making progress.

After being there for an hour, I was now crying and sweating from the pain. The crazy thing was, there was no change in dilation. I have a high pain tolerance, so I knew something was wrong. How close my contractions became—it was apparent that I should have been pushing. They were examining me and the baby over and over, so I knew something was up. Finally, the nurse rushed in and told me that they'd be doing an emergency cesarean. I called my mom, aunt, sister, nana, and they all rushed to the hospital. When they wheeled me to the back, I asked for my mother to be with me. I desperately needed her prayers and comfort more than ever.

Shortly after I woke up, I realized I was in another room. I looked over to see Lust cradling our baby in his arms. Days later, we were able to go home, and I could barely walk. I was literally walking like a slinky because at this point, standing up straight really hurt my incision. All I was focused on was the recovery. With my partner there, I thought it would be an easy recovery—boy, was I wrong!

The first week of recovery, I suffered a setback when my baby girl fell on me, reopening my incision. It ended up being infected. Lust played the PlayStation faithfully, and I tended to the kids with the help of God. Lord knows I was truly in pain. The crazy thing was the jerk knew he wasn't caring for me properly. He said that if he'd have to give himself points—one being the least and ten being the best—he'd give himself a five. I played dumb for so long that I could literally feel the *us* factor coming to an abrupt end. I recovered all the way with the help of God and myself only.

Then I made the hardest decision of my married life—I got my tubes tied so that I'd never produce another amazing person for him again.

I really hated having to always sacrifice what I wanted or didn't want for him. He took pieces away from me that I thought I'd never get back. Lust was always stealing something from me.

CHAPTER 12

The Final Straw

As if Lust hasn't shown me who he was on several occasions, here I was foolishly celebrating our sixth-year wedding anniversary. The whole time, my not-so-significant other was texting many women in a sexual nature. He was slandering the vows we took. Nothing was sacred and never was. Too far was always way too far. I started working my new job the day I found out about it. I really felt like God wanted me to see it. I found it in a strange way because I wasn't looking for it. You see, I had access to his emails, and I was looking for his check stubs that were sent via email. I needed them so I could get a proof of income for childcare. As I was looking for the missing stubs, I found a dating site called Plenty of Fish in his email. It said he hadn't been on in three days. I was like, *Seriously? We just celebrated our anniversary three days ago.*

As soon as I got off from work, I logged on to see text messages agreeing to share himself sexually with other women. There's a saying that I always say. "If you're mine, then you're mine." In other words, if you can be taken away from me, then you weren't mine to begin with. Wasn't that a laugh, considering Lust wasn't mine?

You see, lust could be obtained by anyone who wanted it. It was easily had but hard to get away from. Well, God had really been dealing with me in the midst of it because it was like I was simmering. I could no longer feel Lust, and I stayed angry at his behavior. There would be nights where Lust would want me to respond, but I just couldn't. I couldn't provide Lust with anything. I was disconnected.

I eventually decided to stay committed. I went so far as to say, "No marriage is perfect. I'll get through this."

I continued to struggle with the question, how much was too much for me to take? I didn't want the person I once was to be completely gone. Well, I tried to make changes because I knew either he changes or I'm gone.

Two months later, we moved into our first house. I was so excited about us finally having our own space. I was going to work every day and loving it. Plus, I was getting more and more engrossed in my Bible, and I started to dream more. I loved my dreams because they were like little movie messages from God.

Well, one night, I dreamt that we had split up for good, and I was happy. I thought, *That's not happening because we're good now.* God told me not to share this dream with Lust. I remained quiet and obedient to what I was told, and I never shared this dream with him. Not even a month later, I found Lust cyber cheating again. So I remained quiet. It was like God had my mouth shut. I had peace all around me. The crazy thing was, the following week made seven years of being together—trapped in the dance with Lust.

The next morning, I woke up, still silent and unable to address the situation. We all got in the car together, and this time, I was driving, which was not unusual. Lust was becoming angry with my silence. When we got across town to a red light that was now turning green, Lust jumped out of my car, causing a scene. That was it. I've had it with this foolery. Finally, I found him at the store, and we began talking about what happened. All I could hear was a voice saying, "Guilty," loudly. He lied—pressing his guilt on others. He even went as far as saying that his family member did it from his phone and used his picture. Come on now, really? So he drove off in my car like nothing ever happened. It was the end of my work shift, and he picked me up a little late—like nothing happened. Once we pulled up to the house, he got the kids out. I told him we needed to talk when I get back. I had hair to do, so that was why I wanted to talk to him when I got home.

Once I got home, my mouth just burst out, "I want a divorce."

Lust looked completely shocked like a deer in headlights. I informed him that I was over this chaos between us. On several occasions, he begged me to take him back. Each time, I was unable to produce the words he wanted to hear. God gave me peace of mind with everything and wouldn't let my heart waver. There were many attempts, but it never worked. That's when it hit me—I was set free. Lust was not stuck with me anymore. He no longer had a hold on me. I never stopped dancing. I just changed who I was dancing with. Even the soul tie between us was broken. The funny thing is, when you have made up your mind to let things go, God will do the rest. If God is trying to get to you, he'll remove whatever's in the way to get to you.

CHAPTER 13

Deliverance from Lust

Sometime before Thanksgiving of 2019, I took my children and moved in with my parents. What you see as a step backward was a step forward toward my blessing. I began the process of my divorce, and I was a step closer to being free. I'm not saying Lust never tried to bother me again. I just remind myself with the words, "Resist the devil, and he'll flee." Those words kept me going. I've decided to focus on God and getting closer to him. I'm not perfect, but every day, I am trying. He showed me that I deserve better, so I'll trust and believe in just that.

It was funny how I thought he had already sent *better* on my way, and I was honored to have *better* in my life. I realized God is the only *better* for me, especially at this time. Thank God for *better*, and thank God I'm free!

ABOUT THE AUTHOR

Deandra Evans is a mother of four children. She has always had a passion for writing ever since she was a child. She has joined in UIL Ready Writing contest for school but never wrote her own stories until later in life.

The pen is like a wand, and her mind is the magic. Evans works in childcare and maintains a license in cosmetology, but writing is her first love. She finds it fun to live through the characters she writes about. She would get lost in her writing.

Experiences in life have inspired her to pick her pen up and begin writing again, whether that's to entertain or to just help someone.

CPSIA information can be obtained
at www.ICGtesting.com
Printed in the USA
BVHW031623240122
627018BV00006B/205

9 781639 612444